ABERDEEN

A pictorial souvenir

NESS PUBLISHING

2   The wide, open spaces of Duthie Park.

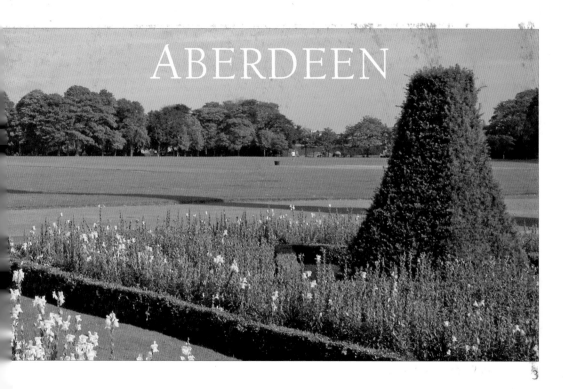

ABERDEEN

Welcome to Aberdeen!

The story of Aberdeen really is a tale of two cities, each one beginning at a riverbank site, eventually uniting and today standing as Scotland's third city. The two settlements developed along very different lines, with 'Old' Aberdeen, close to the River Don, becoming the spiritual and academic heart of north-east Scotland, while 'New' Aberdeen on the Dee was commercially driven, growing into the economic epicentre of the region.

Signs of human occupation in this area are evidenced by many finds dating from 4000BC and earlier, while Tillydrone Motte in Seaton Park has prehistoric origins. The earliest record of a name for the settlements goes back to the Greek geographer Ptolemy in the second century AD, who refers to a place called Devana. His intelligence probably came from Roman incursions around northern Scotland in 84AD. Old Aberdeen's establishment as a sacred centre has its roots in a charming legend. St Machar was advised by St Columba that he would know where to settle when he found a stream shaped like a Bishop's crozier. When Machar reached the River Don and looked down on a U-shaped bend he believed this was the place to which he had been led, so he established a church on that spot, the site now occupied by the cathedral that bears his name. In the fullness of time, the community that grew up around the cathedral earned burgh status, this being conferred in 1489. Six years later Bishop William Elphinstone founded the university. Its first principal was Hector Boece.

Meanwhile, a mile or so to the south, New Aberdeen was exploiting its better harbour at the

An aerial view of Aberdeen looking north. The numbers mark the location of some of the places illustrated in this book and correspond to the relevant page number.

5

mouth of the River Dee and making itself into the premier port in north-east Scotland. Its greater commercial importance helped it acquire burgh status by 1153 at the latest so, paradoxically, in that sense New Aberdeen is much older than Old Aberdeen. The two burghs remained separate until 1891. By 1639 Aberdeen was in fact the second largest city in Scotland after Edinburgh, but in that year it was occupied by five separate armies in quick succession – a consequence of its refusal to sign the National Covenant the previous year.

A few years later, in 1646, a quarter of the population was killed by the plague. The remainder of the 17th century was altogether a difficult time for Aberdeen, but it recovered in the 18th. The discovery of local sources of granite, coupled with a new wave of prosperity, encouraged the city fathers to think and plan big. As a result, from the early 19th century Aberdeen began to take on its distinctive

6   A model of 17th-century Aberdeen which is on display at the Tolbooth Museum, Union Street.

appearance, the unmistakable style of which remains today. The uniformity of the basic building material, worked into a variety of architectural styles, combined effectively to earn the city its epithet of 'The Granite City'. Two architects in particular deserve credit for this achievement, namely Archibald Simpson (1790-1847) and John Smith (1781-1852). The grandiose development of Union Street set the tone, which spread into the adjoining roads and squares, then eventually into the western suburbs.

This book attempts to portray present-day Aberdeen in all its diversity. Starting in the heart of the city at Castlegate, it works its way along Union Street before taking a clockwise loop through Rosemount, Schoolhill and so to King Street, then delves into the harbour area by way of Market Street. A foray into the western suburbs is followed by an exploration of Old Aberdeen before finishing up on the city's coastal rim. Whether the book is read as a visitor's introduction or a resident's souvenir, the visual delights of Aberdeen make for many a fine sight.

The 17th-century Great Hall of Provost Skene's House (see also p.29).

8 Castlegate is the old market place of Aberdeen with markets held since the 12th century. It corresponds to the square in the model shown on p.6. The tall, turreted building is the Salvation Army Citadel.

From the top of the Citadel there is a fine view down Union Street with the Tolbooth steeple (see p.12) 9
and Town House tower visible near the centre. The Mercat (market) Cross is at the bottom of the picture.

10 Back at ground level, the view through the Mercat Cross which also shows some of the fine detail carved on it. It was built in 1686 by John Montgomery and would have replaced an earlier one.

A close-up of the façade of Aberdeen's Town House, built from 1867 to 1873. Most of the earlier Tolbooth **11** (built and enlarged over nearly 200 years from 1629) was demolished to make way for the present structure.

12 Left: the tower of the Town House with 'The Mannie' on the Castlegate Well to the left. Right: a model of the remaining part of the Tolbooth (completed 1629) which is now encased in the Town House.

The magnificent spiral staircase in the Town House, with a statue of Queen Victoria at its base. 13
The statue originally stood in Union Street but was moved into the Town House in 1884.

14 The imposing Town and County Hall in the Town House, venue for a variety of civic functions.

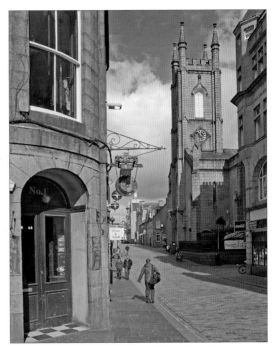

Left: moving west along Union Street reveals Correction Wynd passing beneath. Right: continuing further along Union Street brings us to Belmont Street, which leads to the Art Gallery (see p.27).

16 On the north side of Union Street, between Correction Wynd and Belmont Street, is St Nicholas' churchyard, a popular place for Aberdonians to pass the time on pleasant summer days.

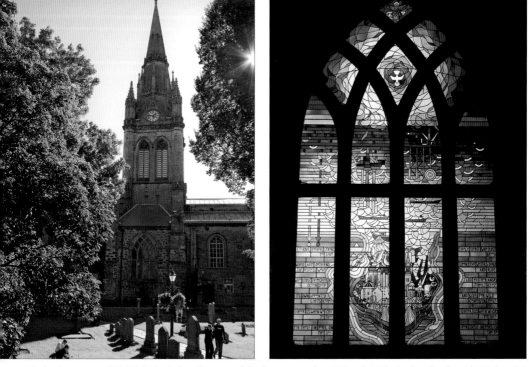

Left: the tower of St Nicholas' church, one of the largest medieval Burgh Kirks in Scotland, with 12th- century origins. Right: since 1990, the transept has housed the Oil Chapel, the window of which is pictured.

18 After Belmont Street, Union Street spans the Denburn valley where Union Terrace Gardens provide a tranquil recreational space in the midst of the city's bustle (see also front cover).

This statue of King Edward VII stands at the junction of Union Street and Union Terrace. **19**
The smaller statues on the side plinths represent some of the former British Dominions.

20 Various styles of residential architecture are found in the roads leading off Union Street. Here we see Bon Accord Crescent where many of the former private houses nowadays find use as commercial premises.

Back on the north side of Union Street, behind the Music Hall, Golden Square forms another 21
enclave of handsome Georgian-style houses, a few of which remain as private homes.

22 Left: the classically colonnaded front of Aberdeen's Music Hall, festooned with Christmas lights.
Right: William Wallace appears to be pointing out the finer points of St Mark's dome!

Just north of Union Street on Rosemount Viaduct the impressive line-up of His Majesty's Theatre, St Mark's Church and the Central Library form a grand and varied view.

24 His Majesty's Theatre was designed by the eminent theatre architect Frank Matcham and opened in 1906. It seats an audience of approximately 1,470.

Opposite the theatre in the triangular space formed by the junction of Union Terrace and **25** Rosemount Viaduct, Christmas lights add another dimension to this nocturnal scene.

26 At the end of Rosemount Viaduct where it meets Schoolhill stands Aberdeen Art Gallery incorporating Cowdray Hall, a popular concert venue, which is lit to good effect on this winter evening.

Aberdeen Art Gallery is one of the city's most popular tourist attractions. A particularly attractive **27** example of late 19th-century architecture, it houses one of the finest art collections in Britain.

28 Behind the Art Gallery is Robert Gordon College. Founded in 1729, the main structure of the 'Auld Hoose' (centre of picture) was completed in 1732, the year after the death of its founder.

Tucked away off Flourmill Lane is Provost Skene's House. Well worth a visit, it is one of Aberdeen's few remaining examples of early burgh architecture, the first reference to which goes back to 1545.

30 Sculpture of water nymphs on the pond in front of Provost Skene's House. Despite appearances, this is actually a night-time shot, complete with an inverted perspective on the house.

Marischal College is the second largest granite building in the world. At the time of preparing this **31** book it was undergoing major work and not looking its best, so this picture is one from its recent past.

32 A short walk up Queen Street from Marischal College leads us to King Street and St Andrew's Episcopal Cathedral. Opened in 1817 as St Andrew's Church, it became a cathedral in the 20th century.

Left: a close-up of the topmost part of the east window at St Andrew's. **33**
Right: statue of the risen Christ on the ciborium in the sanctuary.

34 Union Square, next to the railway station, is Aberdeen's latest shopping mall.
This quirky photograph of its glass frontage reflects the Station Hotel.

Union Square backs on to Market Street, where one is likely to be overlooked by **35** an array of shipping. Aberdeen's harbour comes very close to the city centre.

36 This aerial view illustrates the harbour's layout, with the two main docks to the right and the River Dee to their left. Market Street runs down to the Victoria Bridge, visible in the centre of the picture.

Aberdeen Docks at dawn. Many types of shipping can be seen, although much of it **37** comprises vessels that support the North Sea oil and gas industry.

38 Left: an old capstan on the south side of the harbour and the Round House on the north. Right: the modern Marine Operation Centre, with one facet of its glass cladding reflecting the water below.

More boats line the wharves along the River Dee. Salmon routinely swim through **39** on the way to their spawning grounds on the upper reaches of the Dee.

40 Seen from the Maritime Museum, appropriately located on Shiprow, the Northlink ferry *Hrossey* prepares to sail for the Shetland Isles as a Navy vessel carefully reverses into the dock.

The Maritime Museum tells the story of Aberdeen's long relationship with the sea. It is also the only place 41
in the UK with displays on the North Sea oil and gas industry, such as this huge oil platform model.

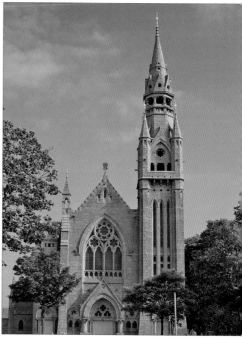

42 Left: The Maritime Museum incorporates Provost Ross's House, which was built in 1593. Right: Queen's Cross Church, dating from 1881, is a fine example of Victorian architecture in Aberdeen's western suburbs.

A short distance along Carden Place from Queen's Cross Church, Albert Drive provides **43** a pleasing view of Aberdeen's residential suburban architecture.

44 Continuing west, this is the Gordon Highlanders' Museum, a vibrant military museum that is home to the regimental treasures of the world-famous Gordon Highlanders. Inset: Saracen armoured car.

Close to the Gordon Highlanders' Museum, off Viewfield Road, here we see 45
Johnston Gardens at their winter best thanks to a hefty fall of snow.

46 In the same part of the city, an aerial view is the best way to see the flooded remains of Rubislaw Quarry, the principal source of the granite used for so many of Aberdeen's buildings.

A little further west we come to Hazelhead Park. The cairns seen here commemorate events 47 in Scotland's history. Inset: detail on the fountain on the right of the main picture.

48 Also in Hazelhead Park is this memorial to the 167 men who lost their lives in the Piper Alpha oil platform disaster of 6th July 1988.

Exploring Aberdeen's parks and gardens leads next to the David Welch Winter Gardens in Duthie Park, one of Europe's largest indoor gardens with many rare and exotic plants on show from all around the world.

50 The superb Victorian Bandstand in Duthie Park. Duthie Park was gifted to the City of Aberdeen by Elizabeth Crombie Duthie in 1880.

She purchased the estate of Arthurseat by the banks of the River Dee for the building and **51** landscaping of the 44-acre park, which opened in 1883. This is the boating lake at sunset.

52 Now we move a couple of miles north to investigate historic Old Aberdeen.
Taken from just within the University grounds, this view looks south down the High Street.

The High Street boasts many fine houses such as this one, College House, built about 1800 on **53** land given by Bishop Gavin Dunbar to the University of Aberdeen in the early 1500s.

54 Aberdeen University was founded in 1495 by Bishop William Elphinstone. The only surviving part of his original buildings is King's College Chapel, the tower of which is on the left in this view.

The interior of King's College Chapel. Built from 1500 to 1509, it possesses one of only two completely intact medieval wooden ceilings that survive in Scottish churches. The other is on p.64!

56 King's College Quad with the Chapel on the right. The Arms of people connected with the University can be seen on the wall, including those of James IV, which are enlarged in the inset picture.

Students make the most of a fine spring day on Elphinstone's lawn. **57**
Elphinstone Hall, completed in 1931, is in the background.

58 Left: the ivy-clad east end of the New King's building, with Kenny Hunter's statue *Youth with a split apple* in the foreground. Right: On College Bounds, the gateway that leads to a house called Powis Gate.

A number of lanes and closes run off the High Street such as this one, 59
Wright's and Cooper's Place, where Old Aberdeen's artisans used to live.

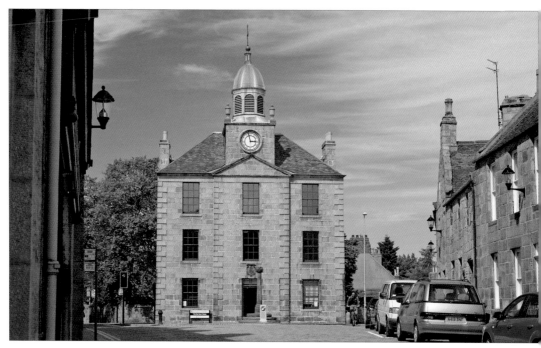

60 At its northern end, the High Street opens out to form a triangular space in front of the Old Town House. The remains of the Market Cross are just visible to the right of the Town House door.

Looking at the view from the 1789-built Old Town House, it's not hard to imagine the **61** market in full swing, making this area the economic hub of the old city.

62 Continuing north by way of The Chanonry, we come to St Machar's Cathedral. Machar was one of Columba's companions and he is attributed with founding a church on this site c.580AD.

The interior of St Machar's, looking towards the east window. It is not known when **63** building commenced, although a date of around 1165 is thought to be probable.

64 As noted above, St Machar's ceiling is an extremely rare survivor and all the more notable for its 48 heraldic shields in three rows of sixteen, nine of which are seen here.

Seaton Park is located immediately north of St Machar's. This is Cathedral Walk at its summer best. **65**

66 In the western corner of Seaton Park stands the Wallace Tower, or more accurately, Benholm's Lodging. It originally stood in Netherkirkgate in the city centre, where Marks & Spencer is now.

The River Don flows to the north of Seaton Park and has been crossed by the Brig o'Balgownie **67** since the late 13th or early 14th century. This is its southern approach.

68 Left: it leads to Balgownie village and was not superseded until construction of the Bridge of Don (right) in 1831, a little further downstream (© Aberdeen City and Shire Regional Identity).

The Aberdeen Exhibition and Conference Centre (AECC) opened in 1985 and more recently underwent an £18 million redevelopment and expansion, making it a truly world-class facility.

70 The Wellington suspension bridge opened in 1831 to cross the River Dee between Ferryhill and Torry. Known locally as the Chain Brig, it has recently undergone a major restoration.

Left: Torry Point lies to the south of Aberdeen. The Battery here was built 1859-1861 to defend the **71** city. From its ruins, the harbour is framed. Right: Girdleness Lighthouse, at the tip of Torry Point.

72 Aberdeen's excellent beach stretches two miles up the coast from the harbour entrance. The seafront is lined with seaside attractions, some of which can be seen in this picture.

74 Seasonal contrasts on Aberdeen beach: left, winter waves and right, summer fun (© Aberdeen City and Shire Regional Identity).

The famous Art Deco Beach Ballroom, a favourite venue for Aberdonians 75
since it first opened its doors in 1929.

76 Whether you stroll along the sand or the esplanade, the beach is always a good place for a walk – weather permitting, of course.

Down by the mouth of the Dee is Foot Dee ('Fittie'), the old fishing village district of the city. **77**

78 Quiz page: where are these? If you need some clues, the following page numbers will point you in the right direction, although they do not necessarily include these items. From top left: 10, 50, 12 (left), 2-3, 11, 25.

And finally: from Tolohill to the south-west of Aberdeen, we see the river spanned by
the Bridge of Dee, with the city spread out beyond.

Published 2010 by Ness Publishing, 47 Academy Street, Elgin, Moray, IV30 1LR
Phone/fax 01343 549663 www.nesspublishing.co.uk

All photographs © Colin and Eithne Nutt except pp.5, 36 & 46 © Scotavia Images; pp.6, 7, 12 (right) & 27 © Aberdeen
Art Gallery & Museums; pp.9, 15 (both), 31, 45 & 51 © Jim Henderson; p.44 (inset) © Gordon Highlanders Museum;
pp.68 (right) & 74 (right) © Aberdeen City and Shire Regional Identity; p.69 © AECC.

Text © Colin Nutt

ISBN 978-1-906549-08-4

Front cover: Union Terrace Gardens; p.1: statue on the Archibald Simpson building; p.4: carving on
Provost Skene's House; this page: Elphinstone memorial, Aberdeen University; back cover: from Castlegate.

For a list of websites and phone numbers please turn over >

Websites and phone numbers (where available) for principal places featured in this book in order of appearance:

Aberdeen: www.aberdeencityandshire.com; www.aberdeencity.gov.uk; www.aboutaberdeen.com
Salvation Army Citadel: www1.salvationarmy.org.uk (T) 01224 579370
Town House and Tolbooth: www.aagm.co.uk
St Nicholas' Church: www.kirk-of-st-nicholas.org.uk (T) 01224 643494
Aberdeen Music Hall: www.musichallaberdeen.com (T) 01224 641122
St Mark's Church: www.stmarksaberdeen.org.uk (T) 01224 640672
His Majesty's Theatre: www.musichallaberdeen.com (T) 01224 641122
Art Gallery: www.aagm.co.uk (T) 01224 523700
Robert Gordon College: www.rgc.aberdeen.sch.uk (T) 01224 646346/646758
Provost Skene's House: www.aagm.co.uk (T) 01224 641086
Marischal College: www.abdn.ac.uk (T) 01224 274301
St Andrew's Cathedral: www.cathedral.aberdeen.anglican.org (T) 01224 640119
Aberdeen Harbour: www.aberdeen-harbour.co.uk (T) 01224 597000
Maritime Museum: www.aagm.co.uk (T) 01224 337700
Queen's Cross Church: www.queenscrosschurch.org.uk (T) 01224 644742
Gordon Highlanders' Museum: www.gordonhighlanders.com (T) 01224 311200